Jesus Loves Me

FIVE SOLAS, FIVE ORGAN ARRANGEMENTS

GRACE CHUNG

JUBAL HOUSE

EXCLUSIVELY DISTRIBUTED BY HAL•LEONARD® CORPORATION

BREHM CENTER

www.jubalhouse.com www.halleonard.com www.brehmcenter.com

SOLA FIDE

The Solid Rock

Lyrics by Edward Mote

My hope is built on nothing less
Than Jesus' blood and righteousness;
I dare not trust the sweetest frame,
But wholly lean on Jesus' name.

On Christ, the solid Rock, I stand:
All other ground is sinking sand,
All other ground is sinking sand.

When darkness veils His lovely face,
I rest on His unchanging grace;
In ev'ry high and stormy gale,
My anchor holds within the veil.

On Christ, the solid Rock, I stand:
All other ground is sinking sand,
All other ground is sinking sand.

His oath, His covenant, His blood
Support me in the whelming flood;
When all around my soul gives way,
He then is all my hope and stay.

On Christ, the solid Rock, I stand:
All other ground is sinking sand,
All other ground is sinking sand.

When He shall come with trumpet sound,
O may I then in Him be found:
Dressed in His righteousness alone,
Faultless to stand before the throne.

On Christ, the solid Rock, I stand:
All other ground is sinking sand,
All other ground is sinking sand.

The Solid Rock
(Sola fide)

Sw. Foundations 8', 4'
Gt. Foundations, Mixtures, Reeds
Ch. Foundations 8', 4', 2'
Ped. 16', 8'

William B. Bradbury
Arr. by Grace Chung

Faster ♩= 116
16
Ch.
simile
19
+ Reeds
23
27

31
Sw.
p
Ch.
f
Sw.
p
35
Ch.
cresc.
39
poco allargando
Brightly ♩ = 96
Gt.
(Solo Reed)
43

47
50
53
7
poco rit.
(Solo)
56
allargando

Sola Scriptura

Jesus Loves Me

Lyrics by Anna B. Warner

Jesus loves me! This I know,
For the Bible tells me so;
Little ones to Him belong,
They are weak but He is strong.

Yes, Jesus loves me!
Yes, Jesus loves me!
Yes, Jesus loves me!
The Bible tells me so.

Jesus loves me! He who died
Heaven's gate to open wide;
He will wash away my sin,
Let His little child come in.

Yes, Jesus loves me!
Yes, Jesus loves me!
Yes, Jesus loves me!
The Bible tells me so.

Jesus loves me! He will stay
Close beside me all the way;
He's prepared a home for me,
And someday His face I'll see.

Yes, Jesus loves me!
Yes, Jesus loves me!
Yes, Jesus loves me!
The Bible tells me so.

Variations on "Jesus Loves Me"
(Sola Scriptura)

Sw. Flutes 8', 2'
Gt. Strings, Flutes 8'
Ped. 16', 8' to balance

William B. Bradbury
Arr. by Grace Chung

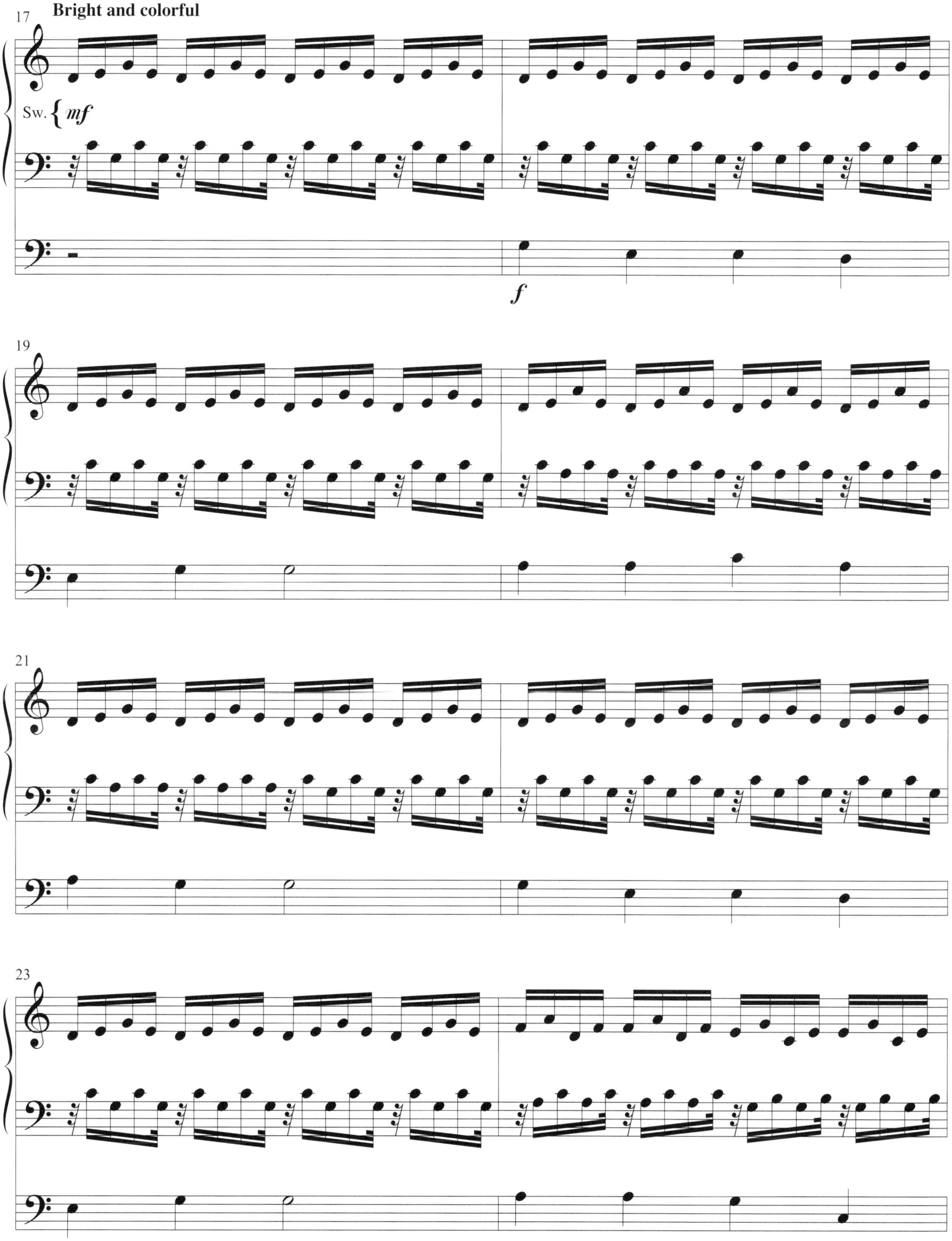
Bright and colorful
Sw.
mf
f
17
19
21
23

25
27
29
31

Jubilantly
mf

45
47
49
Contemplative
Gt.
- 2'
mp
(continue manuals only)
52
55
rit.

58
Stately
gradually building to full organ
mf
62
66
70
f
allargando

Sola Gratia

Come Thou Fount of Every Blessing

Lyrics by Robert Robertson

Come, Thou Fount of every blessing,
Tune my heart to sing Thy grace;
Streams of mercy, never ceasing,
Call for songs of loudest praise.

Teach me some melodious sonnet,
Sung by flaming tongues above;
Praise His name—I'm fixed upon it—
Name of God's redeeming love.

Here I raise my Ebenezer,*
Hither by Thy help I've come;
And I hope, by Thy good pleasure,
Safely to arrive at home.

Jesus sought me when a stranger,
Wandering from the fold of God;
He, to rescue me from danger,
Bought me with His precious blood.

O to grace how great a debtor
Daily I'm constrained to be!
Let Thy goodness, like a fetter,
Bind my wandering heart to Thee:

Prone to wander, Lord, I feel it,
Prone to leave the God I love;
Here's my heart, O take and seal it;
Seal it for Thy courts above.

*Ebenezer: a stone of remembrance (I Samuel 7:12)

Come, Thou Fount of Every Blessing

(Sola gratia)

Sw. Reeds
Gt. Principals 8', 4', 2'
Ch. Principals 8', 4'
Ped. 16', 8'

Traditional American melody
Arr. by Grace Chung

Sw.

21
6
6
6
24
simile
27
30

33
36
Gt.
39
cresc.
42
rit.
+ Reeds

♩ = 88
44
46
48
50

52
54
♩ = 72
ff
56
allargando
59
Sw. + Tpt.
rit.

Solus Christus

Jesus, Lover of My Soul

Lyrics by Charles Wesley

Jesus, Lover of my soul,
Let me to Thy bosom fly,
While the nearer waters roll,
While the tempest still is high;

Hide me, O my Savior, hide,
Till the storm of life is past;
Safe into the haven guide;
O receive my soul at last!

Other refuge have I none;
Hangs my helpless soul on Thee;
Leave, ah! Leave me not alone,
Still support and comfort me.

All my trust on Thee is stayed,
All my help from Thee I bring;
Cover my defenseless head
With the shadow of Thy wing.

Thou, O Christ, art all I want;
More than all in Thee I find;
Raise the fallen, cheer the faint,
Heal the sick and lead the blind.

Just and holy is Thy name,
I am all unrighteousness;
False and full of sin I am,
Thou art full of truth and grace.

Plenteous grace with Thee is found,
Grace to cover all my sin;
Let the healing streams abound;
Make and keep me pure within.

Thou of life the fountain art,
Freely let me take of Thee;
Spring Thou up within my heart,
Rise to all eternity.

Interlude on "Jesus, Lover of My Soul"

(Sola Christus)

Sw. Flutes 8'
Gt. Principals 8', 4'
Ch. Chimes
Ped. 16', 8'

Joseph Parry
Arr. by Grace Chung

17
21
Flowing
Gt.
mp
continue manuals only
24
27
mf
30

33
+ 2'
+ Mixtures
cresc.
36
allargando
39
a tempo
f
gradually building
42

45
48
ff
51
poco allargando
55
sub. p
Ch.

Soli Deo Gloria

To God Be the Glory

Lyrics by Fanny J. Crosby

To God be the glory, great things He hath done!
So loved He the world that He gave us His Son,
Who yielded His life an atonement for sin,
And opened the Lifegate that all may go in.

Praise the Lord, praise the Lord,
Let the earth hear His voice!
Praise the Lord, praise the Lord,
Let the people rejoice!

O come to the Father through Jesus the Son,
And give Him the glory, great things He hath done!

O perfect redemption, the purchase of blood!
To ev'ry believer the promise of God;
The vilest offender who truly believes,
That moment from Jesus a pardon receives.

Praise the Lord, praise the Lord,
Let the earth hear His voice!
Praise the Lord, praise the Lord,
Let the people rejoice!

O come to the Father through Jesus the Son,
And give Him the glory, great things He hath done!

Great things He hath taught us, great things He hath done,
And great our rejoicing through Jesus the Son;
But purer and higher and greater will be
Our wonder, our transport, when Jesus we see.

Praise the Lord, praise the Lord,
Let the earth hear His voice!
Praise the Lord, praise the Lord,
Let the people rejoice!

O come to the Father through Jesus the Son,
And give Him the glory, great things He hath done!

To God Be the Glory
(Soli Deo gloria)

Sw. Solo Reed 8'
Gt. Principals 8', 4', 2', Mixtures
Ch. Principals 8', 4', 2'
Ped. 16', 8'

WILLIAM H. DOANE
Arr. by Grace Chung

Joyfully ♩ = 92

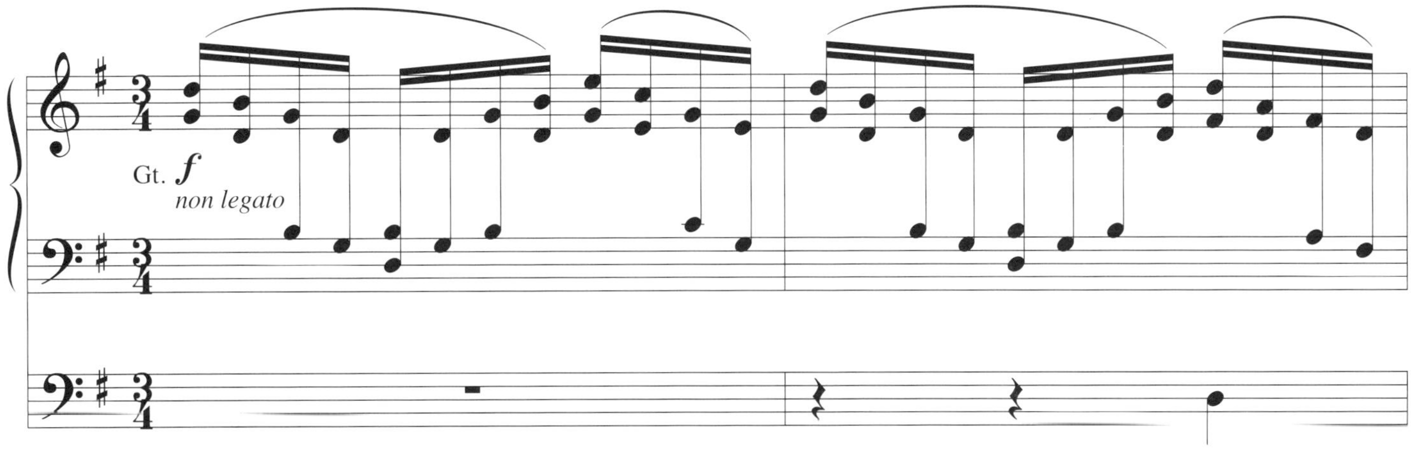

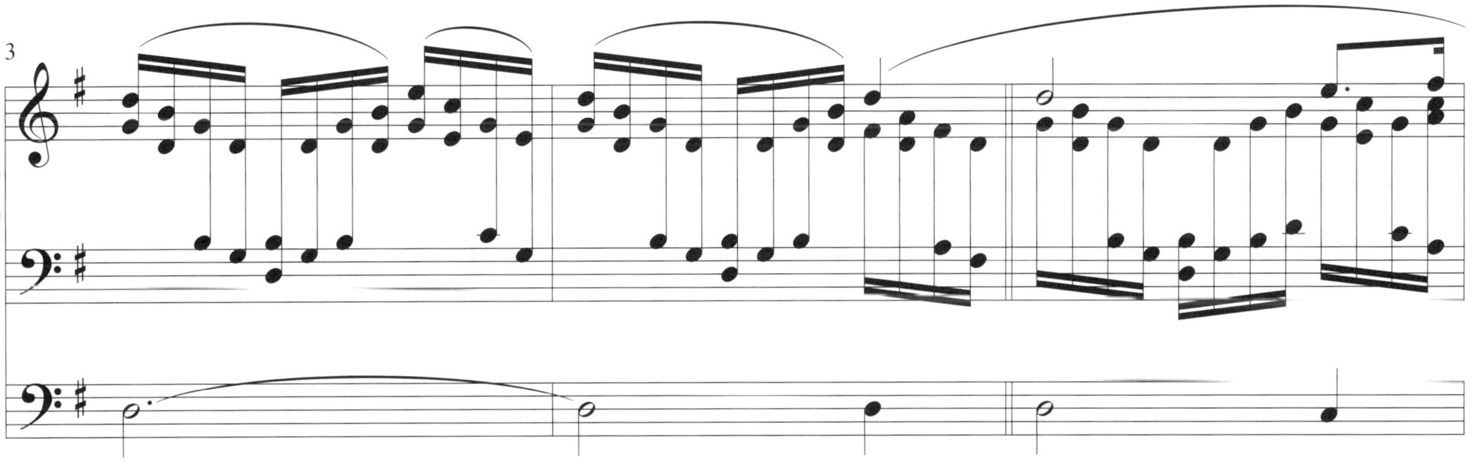

9
12
15
18

21
Ch.
Gt.
24
Ch.
Gt.
27
30

Ch.
Solo 8' Reed

(♩ = 𝅗𝅥)
45
48
51
54

57
60
(♩ = ♩)
Sw. Tpts.
f
63
66

69
Gt.
Gt.
72
Ped. Full with Reeds
75
78

81
84
87
90
(Full)

94
98
103
rit.
a tempo
3
107
+ Reeds

semper reformanda

THE FIVE SOLAS PROJECT

Resources in the Five Solas Music project are:

Five songs for children's choir based on the five sola themes:

- **WE BELIEVE (CREED)** – Faith Alone
- **DEEP, DEEP LOVE OF JESUS** – Christ Alone
- **GRACE, GOD'S GRACE** – Grace Alone
- **O WORD OF GOD (SO STRONG AND TRUE)** – Scripture Alone
- **GLORY BE TO GOD** – Glory to God Alone

Listening CD, stereo and split tracks, and chord charts are available.

There is a Five Solas Resource Pak for directors/teachers. The resource pak includes stories, responsive readings, devotional guides with discussion questions, and copyable activities to enhance the experience of focusing on each of the five sola themes.

Also for children and teachers/parents is a fully illustrated storybook, **GROWING GOD'S WAY**. The five stories invite an imaginative look at each of the sola themes. A music CD is included to further enhance the storytelling experience.

GRACE ALONE is a book of five choral pieces for adult choir that highlights the sola themes using historic texts. Optional orchestrations for both full and chamber instrumentations are available, as well as a listening CD. Responsive readings are also available as complimentary downloads from the website.

LIFT HIGH THE CROSS and **JESUS LOVES ME** are collections of piano and organ solos, respectively, that focus attention on the sola themes. These artistic offerings are intended to challenge pianists and organists musically, while at the same time providing creative keyboard resources for worship.